STONER TROLL UNDER THE BRIDGE

Written and Illustrated by
D E Pownell

For Mom

Copyright © 2017. All rights reserved. Published by D E Pownell. Many thanks to: Shawn, Lori, Scot and Dawn. Also thank you to Mark, Rachael and all my friends and family for their continued support and understanding. A very special thanks to Winston for that walk in the park.
www.stonertroll.com

ISBN: 978-0-692-86281-0

Sally and Timmy loved walking to school.
In the spring when it's damp and in the fall when it's cool.

They passed through a park, all lovely and green.
They played in the meadow and splashed in the stream.

The stream in the park
        would meander and twist,

And sometimes, in the morning,
        it displayed quite a mist.

There was a bridge that crossed over,
      which started their day.

It was a great place to run and a great place to play.

When they reached the spot
		where the bridge should be,

The fog was so thick that they just couldn't see.

"Maybe a skunk has died,"
said Timmy quite sadly,

"The smell is so strong it must have died very badly."

The fog was so thick
 and it seemed to get thicker.

It made them feel sick,
 and they seemed to get sicker.

Then one quiet morning,
     as they went skipping along,

There was, not quite a mist,
     but something more like a fog.

They stood at the foot of their bridge rather puzzled.
From under the bridge there was a cough that seemed muzzled.

"Who is under the bridge, making such a horrible sound?
Is it a man who smokes cigarettes? They are bad!" Timmy frowned.

"Oh NO!" cried Sally,
   "This is not some guy smoking!"

"This is worse, my dear Timmy.
   This is a troll who is toking!"

"What's sup?" said the troll.
"Got any food?" he said sickly.

"NO, we do not!" said Sally quite prickly.

Cough, cough!! The troll gagged,
"Yeah, ok, so that's cool."

"What's cool?" demanded Sally,
"Now we need to get to school!"

"Yeah, okay," said the troll,
    "But can you talk slower man?"

"What?" replied Sally,
    "We can't see the bridge from the land."

The troll mumbled something, making no sense.

"Are you okay?" asked Sally. "Should I call an ambulance?"

"NO, NO!" cried the troll,
      "I don't need that kinda shit!"

"I'm good, it's all good,"
      as he took one more hit.

The children waited and waited, trying to see through the fog.

"I thought I had one," asked the troll,

"but man, where's my dog?"

"This is crazy!" cried the children, "The air is not getting better!"

"It's okay," said the troll,

"I think he's wearing a sweater."

"Oh no," pleaded Sally. "What a terrible fate."

"We are going to the science museum and now we'll be late."

The troll, he continued, "Science is everywhere man."
"From like a tiny little rain drop that falls in your hand."

"Like the drop holds the weather,"
                    proclaimed the troll rather proudly.

"What, that is crazy!" shouted the children quite loudly.

"Got any change?"
 asked the troll, his voice starting to dim.

Timmy looked in his pockets,
 but Sally stopped him.

Finally Sally said firmly,
"This guy is a fool."

"If we hop on the rocks we can make it to school."

So, they hopped on the rocks with no splashes, what luck!

Sally leading the way and Timmy thinking,
Poor skunk.

www.ingramcontent.com/pod-product-compliance
Lightning Source LLC
Chambersburg PA
CBHW082249300426
44110CB00039B/2490